An opinio

CW01512981

MAKE LONDON

Written by
RIYA PATEL

County Hall Pottery (no.26)

INFORMATION IS DEAD.
LONG LIVE OPINION.

When we conceived these guidebooks, we feared they would fail. Who needs a guidebook when everything can be googled for free?

But then it occurred to us; that's exactly why you *do* want a guidebook. You want lively, trustworthy opinion combined with great photographs. You don't want endless information from a thousand online bots.

We think you are like us: you care about quality, you care about style, you care about provenance, but you don't have time to waste on long words like 'provenance'. You want to cut to the chase: where's good?

If you were to come and stay on our couch (it's a metaphor btw; we have a guide to hotels), these are the places we'd recommend.

Ann & Martin, co-founders
Hoxton Mini Press

Cone8 Ceramics Studio (no.11)
Opposite: Yussico (no.23)

JamJar Edit (no.36)

London Centre for Book Arts (no.6)
Opposite: Gather (no.27)

MADE IN LONDON

What can you learn to make in London? Well, an awful lot actually. This city has a rich history of craftsmanship dating back to Roman times, when jewellery, ceramics, pottery, glass-making and metalwork thrived here. During the medieval era, powerful guilds of goldsmiths, clothworkers and iron-mongers practically ran the capital's economy. We may have come a long way since then, but London's craft scene remains an unstoppable force.

Keeping this heritage alive are professional crafters of all stripes, from bookbinders to bread-makers, weavers to whittlers. Not only are they committed to slow making, but often more than happy to share their skills. Lots of the classes in this guide take place in working studios, where teachers juggle their own work while showing beginners the ropes. Some are among the best (or only) craftspeople to continue a historic practice.

If there were ever a subject that needed a guidebook, this is it. Traditionally, the smell, noise and mess of making have kept it at the city's edges; now sky-high rents push most hubs even further to London's peripheries. On this odyssey of over 50 crafts, I've poked my nose into shop attics, old warehouses, garden workshops, church basements and railway arches to find makers and making communities. Put your faith in Google Maps and you'll open doors to parts of this town you never knew existed – from the London School of Mosaic (no.50), found under a bog-standard housing estate, to the Flower Appreciation Society (no.48), occupying a magical back-street courtyard that feels far too bucolic for its urban Dalston setting.

But why bother making something yourself in this age of easy consumption? Sustainability credentials aside, the answer is simple: to get out of your comfort zone and surprise yourself. The day I tried blacksmithing at Boneyard London (no.40), I woke up sick with worry that I might brand myself with a hot poker – but I emerged unscathed and with a brilliant sense of accomplishment. I've had some soothing, eye-opening, terrifying and exhilarating experiences while writing this book – none of which could have happened through a screen. Keep up your new skill and you might reach craft nirvana: the kind of mind-and-body harmony others find at the gym or night-club. And it's sociable, too; in the words of Slipstitch's (no.47) Rosie Fletcher, 'Craft is just a front for making friends.'

Pass by Threadneedle Street, Tanner's Yard or Iron-monger Row and you'll be reminded that crafts of all sorts are indelibly written upon this great city. This opinionated guide urges you to give some of them a try.

Riya Patel
London, 2025

Riya is an editor, writer and proud south Londoner who's travelled the world reporting for magazines including Icon, Frame *and* Crafts.

BEST FOR...

Mindfulness

'I thought this was supposed to be relaxing' is a common refrain among fraught beginners tackling crafts. The truth is that some are more taxing to get started in than others. At the peaceful Turning Earth studios (no.49), you can get hands on with ceramics in a laid-back environment. Meanwhile, snipping blades of straw with Kim Jordan (no.20) is so focused that you'll be sure to find your zen.

Couples

Date on the horizon? Do something more meaningful with your sweetheart than visiting a forgettable bar or restaurant. A kintsugi class with Kinboru (no.15) is all about making strong, beautiful bonds. You can exchange handmade tokens of affection at Ringsmiths (no.32). And 58 and CO's gin school (no.18) is the place to head for some (literal) Dutch courage.

Short on time

Not everyone has an entire day to dedicate to craft mastery. Get a quick creative fix at Paper Stories (no.34), the drop-in collage cafe. Swing by Earl of East (no.42) to make a scented candle and shop on Regent Street while it sets. And at action-filled glassblowing studio Gather (no.27), you can come out with a drinking vessel in just an hour.

Small budgets

There's no getting away from it: learning a craft can be eye-wateringly expensive. Art4Space (no.35) has experienced tutors running low-priced classes. Quilt Club (no.54) is a community of textile-lovers sharing skills (and snacks) for free. Pigment Press (no.41) runs free kids' printing workshops in the school holidays, but *shhh* – keep that one to yourself before places get snapped up.

Obsessives

Need to know everything about your niche subject? Luckily London has a lot of passions covered. Discover bread in detail at E5 Bakehouse (no.13), ask experts at St Bride Foundation (no.3) all you've ever wanted to know about printing or get to grips with how frames are made in the studious lab of eyewear specialist Cubitts (no.52).

Families

Stop small (and big) hands from endlessly scrolling by checking out a family-friendly class or craft destination. Tufting can be fun for teens – find it at Tufting London (no.22) or Fulham Textile Studio (no.44) – while parents can sculpt clay with their kids at pottery studio Cone8 (no.11). Put the welcoming Blackhorse Workshop (no.8) on your map for SEN-friendly woodwork clubs and family discos.

1

MAYA NJIE

Discover your signature scent

If you've ever dreamt of bottling a memory, self-taught perfumier Maya Njie can help you tune into your scent associations through an extensive session of 'blind smelling'. Fragrant fun ensues as you try to guess 15 different sources used in perfumery. You'll learn historical facts, ethical talking points and the science of blending top, heart and base notes. Along with fruity and floral odours, there are some surprisingly disgusting aromas: ambergris (vomited up by whales) and pungent civet (from a cat's bottom) are two that stick in the nostrils. Once you've discovered what floats your olfactory boat, you'll sniff, swirl and blend your way to a bespoke formula to take home.

91A Rivington Street, EC2A 3AY
Nearest station: Shoreditch High Street
mayanjie.com

2

CLUNIE FRETTON

Turn blocks of wood into works of art

A couple of hours spent in master carver Clunie's studio will give you a new appreciation for furniture and buildings that sport intricate, ornamental wood. In her small-group taster class, you'll learn how to 'chip carve' decorative patterns in a block of soft lime wood by using sharp chisels to scoop out the surface, bit by bit. Some find their groove straight away; others have a frustrating time getting a handle on the technique. If you're struggling, take time to look around at Clunie's impressive work for historic cathedrals and museums. She'll reassure you that her first attempts looked no different to yours when she started her carving journey ten years ago.

Cockpit Bloomsbury, Cockpit Yard,
Northington Street, WC1N 2NP
Nearest stations: Chancery Lane, Holborn
cluniefretton.com

3

ST BRIDE FOUNDATION

Print a poster using archive type

Read all about it! Three veterans of the newspaper trade will help you create a letterpress poster in a day at this former social club for Fleet Street printers. Bring a quote of up to 12 words, select the perfect blocks of type to make it shout and they'll show you how to set them, ink them up and roll paper over them, working towards a crisp final edition. St Bride is a real piece of London's print history, where tales and terminology from the pre-digital days hover around a workshop filled with antique presses and old newsprint. When you hang up your apron at the end of the day, you'll feel like you've clocked off a shift from yesteryear.

14 Bride Lane, EC4Y 8EQ
Nearest station: City Thameslink
sbf.org.uk

4

TEA AND CRAFTING

Light-hearted classes for craft-starters

Bedecked with strings of fluffy pom-poms, shredded paper tassels, polka dot tablecloths and trays full of cupcakes, if you're not already here for a hen-do, you'll certainly get in the party spirit in this bubbly space above the throngs of Covent Garden. For the craft-curious it's an easy-going place to bring friends for a bash at lino-printing, calligraphy, macramé and more. Crafts are just a notch of difficulty above those you may have already tried at home or school and there's a packed calendar to explore. Leave your inner perfectionist at home and enjoy the process in these lively and light-hearted classes taught in groups of ten.

15 Maiden Lane, WC2E 7NG
Nearest station: Charing Cross
teaandcrafting.co.uk

5

DALIA JAMES

Weave your worries away

Explore tapestry with artist Dalia James, who's renowned for her Mondrian-like grids of colour. It's meditative, tactile and weirdly addictive – like painting, but with texture. Using yarn that she hand-dyes in exquisite jewel tones, she'll show you how to set up a frame loom – the hobby-friendly type that can happily sit in your lap at the kitchen table. Weaving the yarn (known as the 'weft') between vertical threads (the 'warp'), you'll criss-cross your way to a mini tapestry, learning methods of plain weave, dovetail and hatch. Candy-floss strands of unspun yarn ('roving') can be knotted and plaited in, too. Inspired to become a home weaver? You'll be pleased to know that this is one craft where all the kit can be made or bought for very little.

Cockpit Bloomsbury, Cockpit Yard,
Northington Street, WC1N 2NP
Nearest stations: Chancery Lane, Holborn
daliajames.com

6

LONDON CENTRE FOR BOOK ARTS

Build the skills to bind your own book

The sound of sharp blades shearing through paper lets you know a class is in progress at this mecca for print lovers. On the comprehensive four-part bookbinding course, you'll work up from a simple pamphlet to a clothbound volume, learning how to craft concertinas and Japanese stab-binding along the way. It's a highly technical course, but knowledgeable tutors give good guidance and can advise on personal projects, too. Getting the sections in order can require some mental gymnastics, but keeping a neat bench aids a clear mind. On your break, explore the incredible collection of vintage equipment, books and paraphernalia here – amassed thanks to co-founder Simon Goode's obsession with print history and persistent eBay habit.

Britannia Works, 56 Dace Road, E3 2NQ
Nearest station: Hackney Wick
londonbookarts.org

7

PRINT CLUB LONDON

Personalised professional screen prints

However eager you are to get your hands inky, the trick to successful screen printing is not rushing the prep. Turn up with a digital artwork and Print Club will demystify the process of making a print in a day, from setting an image up in Photoshop to exposing it onto an emulsion-coated screen using UV light. After lunch, you'll make friends with a specialist printing bed (each has a name), which will suck your paper flat and clamp your screen in place, helping avoid any pesky misalignment. Firmly pull a single gloopy colour over the screen and voilà! Your print is underneath on weighty A4 paper. It's an immensely satisfying process and you'll wish you had more time to spend here.

Unit 3, 10–28 Millers Avenue, E8 2DS
Nearest station: Dalston Kingsland
printclublondon.com

8

BLACKHORSE WORKSHOP

Inclusive hub for learning wood and metalcraft

Fancy sand-casting a bronze amulet, lathe-turning a candlestick or joining a feminist welding club? This welcoming wood and metal workshop will help you find your thing. Its aim is to share making skills more widely, with SEN-friendly kids' wood-work clubs and concessionary class rates being some of the inclusive and affordable ways to get involved. The community spirit is strong within this rough-and-ready collection of corrugated metal buildings and old shipping containers, and those who try a class often come back for more. Drop by the cafe, which doubles as an exhibition space, or join a free family disco in the yard. This is the kind of makers' paradise you wish every postcode would have.

1–2 Sutherland Road Path, E17 6BX
Nearest station: Blackhorse Road
blackhorseworkshop.co.uk

9

THE NEW CRAFT HOUSE

Stitch a bespoke brassiere

If you've ever been tempted to make your own bra, friends Hannah Silvani and Rosie Scott can show you the ins and outs of underwires at their deadstock fabric shop. The place is like a giant pick-and-mix, packed to the rafters with rolls and remnants. In a tiny classroom, you'll use a top spec Pfaff machine to run up a bespoke brassiere in an intimate group of eight fellow sewists. The atmosphere here is warm and friendly but studious, with copious note-taking going on to keep up with the many stages. To get a feel for the experience, tune in to Hannah and Rosie's effervescent podcast of the same name, where they tell all about running a sustainable craft business.

32 Bocking Street, E8 3FP
Nearest station: London Fields
thenewcrafthouse.com

10

THE GREEN WOOD GUILD

An ultra-sustainable ancient skill

Wood whittling is a sociable craft that's easy for beginners, enrapturing many who come to try it among the grazing sheep of Stepney City Farm. Take an intro class with the guild's legendary founder, Barn the Spoon, and you can come back for Spoon Club – a weekly untaught session for members. Unlike seasoned timber, the moisture in green wood makes it soft, flexible and pleasing to carve into characterful spoons and bowls. With the correct knife grips, you can sit and safely work a piece in your hands, shaving away as butter-like curls of blond wood pile up at your feet. Materials are an ever-changing mix of what's local and available, from Kentish sweet chestnut to fallen London street trees.

Stepney City Farm, Stepney Way, E1 3DG
Nearest stations: Stepney Green, Limehouse
thegreenwoodguild.com

11

CONE8 CERAMICS STUDIO

Play with clay

Give form to your wildest ideas at Cone8, where experimentation is encouraged and everything from erotic candlesticks to keepsake sea urchins have emerged from its kilns. You will learn how to develop your personal style, which can feel like motivational therapy as much as craft. Energetic co-founder KC acts as a self-confessed hype woman, guiding private sessions or small groups of six. Her Asian cultural heritage and sound technical expertise inform the programme, which includes classes in coloured clay, allowing potters to explore swirling, marbling and overlaying patterns freely. Weekly family sessions that celebrate children's playful creativity are a core part of the studio's ethos.

Studio 84, Adansbeck Court, 33 Rookwood Way, E3 2XT
Nearest station: Hackney Wick
coneeight.co.uk

12

NEW SCHOOL OF FURNITURE MAKING

Make a simple three-legged stool in a day

If woodwork gives you the horrors rather than happy thoughts, be assured that almost anyone can make this stool in a day. Pleasingly simple, it has a pre-made pine top, beech legs and rails that fit together with a series of round mortise and tenon joints. If you bodge it, there are plenty of workarounds – from sanding away rough bits to starting parts over. The drilling, sawing and finishing is mostly done by hand rather than noisy machine, so you can spend the hours bonding with your bench-mates. With a sturdy lightweight stool to call your own, you'll emerge buoyant – even if you attract strange looks taking it home on the bus.

4 Beechwood Road, E8 3DY
Nearest station: Dalston Junction
newschooloffurniture.com

13
E5 BAKEHOUSE

Rise to the challenge of baking sourdough

E5's marathon full-day class involves learning the steps for no less than four types of sourdough: seeded bagels, ciabatta-style rolls, rye and a country loaf. Amid the hubbub of the cafe and pro bakers wheeling trolleys of hot loaves around, you'll measure out each dough, mix, rest, prove, stretch and shape it – and, finally, slide it into industrial ovens for the perfect bake. Bread-heads will devour the obsessive knowledge offered here. If you've just a mild interest, the science-y bits can feel like a school lesson, but you'll come home laden with baked goods and well fed with E5 fare (a freshly prepared breakfast spread, lunch and pastries are all included).

396 Mentmore Terrace, E8 3PH
Nearest station: London Fields
e5bakehouse.com

14

CROWN WORKS POTTERY

Convivial clay crafting

Across a courtyard strung with festoon lights, this cosy studio invites would-be potters to gather round huge tables as if at a dinner party. On its two-hour hand-building taster, you'll roll out a slab of clay like a giant piece of pastry or playdoh, cutting out and curling a rectangle to create a mug or pot, to which you add a bottom and handle. The table is laid with pots of intriguing tools, each perfect for producing a particular decorative effect. Rubber kidneys smooth surfaces (an addictive, meditative process), rollers leave a textured imprint and wire loops are there for scooping out facets. Time is tight, so it helps to come with an idea for your design beforehand.

11-12 Crown Works, Temple Street, E2 6QQ
Nearest station: Cambridge Heath
crownworkspottery.com

15

KINBORU STUDIOS

Perfectly imperfect pottery

Kintsugi isn't just a craft, it's a whole life philosophy. The ancient Japanese art of mending broken ceramics with gold and lacquer represents embracing life's imperfections. In an accelerated, modern take on this, Kinboru's Brandon Le leads a group of 14 through the process of smashing a pot and putting it back together. His jokey banter keeps the experience light-hearted. You squeeze epoxy resin on to the breaks, hold them together then flick at the join with fine gold powder, which also dusts your face and hair with a disco sheen. If you can't catch Brandon for help as he dashes around, get friendly with your fellow classmates, who can hopefully step in to troubleshoot.

Buckle Street Studios by Locke, 21 Buckle Street, E1 8DB
Nearest station: Aldgate East
Other locations: Peckham, Southwark
kinboru.com

16

POPHAMS HOME

Artistic pursuits at a foodie favourite

Famed for doing revolutionary things with hand-crafted pastry, this bakery's founders have a love of making things from scratch. This extends to the timber-clad home store beside its Hackney branch (a country-style haven of rustic pots and raw linen) and a rolling programme of classes in the dedicated space above. Squeezed under its fondant-pink ceiling arch, you'll get the uncanny feeling of being inside a Pophams confection itself. Many of the UK artisans whose items appear in the shop and bakeries are part of the teaching line-up. Come for an enlightening session of pinch pottery, lost wax casting or leathercraft, or join for a casual collage-and-wine Wednesday.

197 Richmond Road, E8 3NJ
Nearest station: London Fields
pophamshome.com

17

LONDON TERRARIUMS

Self-enclosed green worlds

Tinyjohns, fittonias, carboys... the world of terra-riums has its own amusing lingo, whether in reference to the glass vessel in which you make your miniature garden or the tiny plants that fill it. Emma Sibley, friendly plant expert and author, will let you in on the process of making and caring for one, and shares the fascinating history of the 19th-century craze for growing humidity-loving plants under glass. Once you've filled a container with gravel and soil, you'll use long tweezers and a cork on a stick to drop in and bed down your chosen greenery. You'll feel positively godlike as you hover over the tiny world you have created. No wonder Londoners lacking garden space love making these little botanical marvels.

139 Bethnal Green Road, E2 7DG
Nearest station: Shoreditch High Street
Other location: Deptford
londonterrariums.com

18

58 AND CO

Make like a moonshiner

Banned in the 18th century for causing widespread debauchery in the city, small-batch gin distillation is back on the right side of the law. In a secluded Haggerston railway arch, 58 and CO helps you blend tangy juniper with a huge choice of botanicals (tonka beans, cranberries, cocoa husks and more). A little flavour goes a long way here. Heat your ingredients with a base spirit in a miniature copper still and wait for the resulting vapours to drip out. You'll end up with a 70cl bottle of gin that you get to name and seal with wax. This premium experience will definitely get you tipsy: it includes three cocktails, several spirits to sip and – mercifully – snacks to soak it all up.

329 Acton Mews, E8 4EF
Nearest station: Haggerston
58andco.com

19

WAX ATELIER

Hand-dip candles using natural wax

Long and tapered, fat and stubby or twisted around each other romantically, hand-dipped candles are a sensory treat – and that's before you get into the myriad possibilities of wax types, scents and natural dyes. Wax Atelier will show you how to make yours by repeatedly building up layers of creamy plant-based wax or beeswax on a string. The trick is to keep your body relaxed and your dipping quick: any jerky movements will create bumps. This simple craft is a bit like cooking, with the same recipe coming out differently depending on the maker. Follow the studio on Instagram for its latest workshops, as they occur ad hoc around their small-batch production runs and activities for the local community.

Unit E, Sutherland House, Sutherland Road, E17 6BJ
Nearest station: Blackhorse Road
Other locations: various, see website
waxatelier.com

20

KIM JORDAN

Make meditative patterns with straw

Straw marquetry is a luxe French craft so pains-taking that prisoners of the Napoleonic war would do it to fill their time. Ultra-patient furniture designer Kim Jordan picked up the decorative technique in Paris a decade ago, put a modern spin on it and now teaches it in his snug canal-side workshop. Over three hours, he'll show you how to apply thin strips of glossy, colourful straw to a postcard-sized base, leaving a mesmerising finish as the light catches each piece differently. Learn to slit open the straw, flatten it with a bone folder, then cut and glue sections into your chosen pattern. A truly meditative experience if you're in the right mindset.

Hone London, 16 Pixley Street, E14 7DF
Nearest station: Limehouse
kimjordan.co.uk

21

THE LONDON EMBROIDERY STUDIO

Sew bespoke art in sequins, beads and thread

Keen embroiderers, this is your chance to learn from the best and master the art of embellishment while discovering its therapeutic joy. This pro studio is deft at couture-level embroidery for major fashion houses, as well as costumes for film, TV and stage (bits of Joseph's technicolour dreamcoat have been found scattered around these cutting tables). All are welcome at its playful hand-embroidery taster sessions, where you'll learn the basics of running stitches, chains and knots in a kaleidoscopic palette of threads. A week-long summer school aimed at career-starters unravels the workings of machine embroidery, too. Here, you'll be encouraged to explore your individual style as you take a design from paper to stitch.

38 Ermine Mews, Laburnum Street, E2 8BF
Nearest station: Haggerston
londonembroiderystudio.com

22
TUFTING LONDON

Fluffy rug-making for the trigger-happy

Rug tufting is a kitsch craze that's sweeping China, an easy-to-learn craft that lends itself to bright colours and emoji-like designs that are made even cuter with a shaggy texture. After a surprisingly stern health and safety briefing, you're shown how to shoot loops of yarn through canvas using a tufting gun with a series of satisfying little bangs. The gun automatically cuts the wool on the other side, making the process fast, noisy and excellent fun. You'll make a rug of your own design, while an upbeat pop soundtrack gets you in the swing. After a while, your shooting arm will ache, so don't be afraid to ask the pros to help blast through your piece to finish in time.

Unit A, 10 Hebden Place, SW8 2FR
Nearest station: Nine Elms
tuftinglondon.com

23

YUSSICO

A holistic way to work with leather

This comprehensive half-day class starts with studying leather under a microscope. Passionate leathercraft advocate Yusuf Osman explains how the material's structural quirks will tell you how it wants to be plied. In groups of just four in his pin-neat studio, he'll guide you in making two accessories from a choice of purse, pencil case or key ring. You'll master cutting patterns from soft, strong and colourful hides while learning the culture of the trade. Cut carefully, as there are no hems to hide mistakes. After folding and fixing everything with smart brass fittings, you can mark your accoutrement with your initials or those of a loved one (this is a perfect activity for a leather wedding anniversary).

Cockpit Deptford, 18–22 Creekside, SE8 3DZ
Nearest station: Deptford
yussi.co

24

LONDON STONE CARVING

Chip and chisel a stone leaf over a weekend

Just as you're questioning Google Maps for sending you into the bowels of an Asda car park off the Old Kent Road, you'll stumble upon this magical Michelangelo's atelier. Founded by four mates who honed their skills at nearby City & Guilds of London Art School, this is a working studio where you're surrounded by sculpted busts and intricate reliefs. Workshops are for anyone aged 15–60 and a refreshingly non-stuffy approach encourages the curious to simply 'have a go'. Over a weekend, you'll get hands on with tools to set up, rough out and carve a classical oak leaf from Portland Stone to take home. Be quick to sign up: courses only happen every couple of months.

52 Ossory Road, SE1 5AN
Nearest station: South Bermondsey
londonstonecarving.com

25

MARMOR PAPERIE

Chat, splat and play with paper patterns

In her popular introductory class, London's only pro marbler Lucy McGrath will take you through a fun and fast-paced few hours. After a quick history lesson that includes the craft's ancient roots through to its revival in the Instagram era, it's time to get started. You can try out seven patterns made by floating acrylic paint on water, creating blobs, swirls and flourishes by using a comb, skewer or flick of a brush. Prepare to get splattered as bright colours and metallics fly across the table and creative juices flow: her lively course demands you get messy. Lucy will post you your finished papers, and you can even have your favourites made into a bespoke notebook – she is also a keen bookbinder.

Cockpit Deptford, 18-22 Creekside, SE8 3DZ
Nearest station: Deptford
marmorpaperie.co.uk

26
COUNTY HALL POTTERY

Throw pots in an iconic location

County Hall lives a bizarre multiple life as the home of two hotels, London's only aquarium, the set of an Agatha Christie play and now a working pottery. It's run by a pair of intrepid ceramicists who have turned various spots in this labyrinthine building into a classroom, gallery and shop, bringing it a new creative status. You can learn to throw a pot on a wheel here, but know that it's unlikely you'll be able to master the skill in one morning. What you will get is firm but friendly advice on keeping a strong body position to control the clay and help finding a technique that suits you. If things go wrong, there's no embarrassment here – should your lump go spinning off and hit the floor, the team will discreetly hand you a new one.

County Hall, Belvedere Road, SE1 7GP
Nearest station: Waterloo
countyhallpottery.com

27

GATHER

Alchemical glassblowing

If you can stand the hellish heat of Gather's furnaces – which are kept at an extreme 1,175°C – the reward is a spectacular speckled vessel of your own making. On the studio's intense one-hour taster class, you're handed a pipe with a blob of plain molten glass on the end, which you roll through coloured glass chips that adhere and melt into your piece during a blast in the furnace. With intervals of just minutes to work while the glass is malleable, you're helped to form it using sodden paper, moulds, tools and – the really fun bit – your own breath, by blowing down the pipe. There's lots to do simultaneously (including staying cool), but you'll be in safe hands the whole time.

Unit 4, Submarine Cable Depot,
Warspite Road, SE18 5NX
Nearest station: Woolwich Dockyard
gather.glass

28
THE FAN MUSEUM

Make your own Georgian accessory

If there were a prize for the prettiest setting, this Greenwich museum would be a top contender. Its orangery is a piece of bonafide Georgian history and it's here, surrounded by hand-painted murals, a chequerboard floor and fancy French doors, that you'll learn to make two types of fan using your own paper. Sip tea from a china cup while getting to grips with the lollipop-like cockade and traditional folding fan; both accessories were the height of fashion when this neighbourhood was built. It's a shame there's not more time for history, because this whirlwind class requires you to get straight down to the tricky business of pleating paper. You'll need to be precise – there's not much room for error in this exacting process.

12 Crooms Hill, SE10 8ER
Nearest station: Greenwich
thefanmuseum.org.uk

29

FREEWEAVER STUDIO

Mindful space for intuitive weaving

The piles of raw fleece and gently clacking wooden looms in this peaceful studio will make you forget you're in a busy capital city. On a hand-built free-standing loom that's already set up, you'll be shown how to run up long piece of fabric in just a few hours. There's no plan or pattern to follow; you work by choosing from textured yarns, fluffy merino and strips of recycled sari fabric, which – for the indecisive – presents the main challenge. Once body and mind get in the rhythm of working the loom and passing a shuttle (the tool that carries the yarn) back and forth, intuition takes over and you'll find yourself in the perfect state of flow. You can keep your resulting woven piece as a wall hanging, or sew it into a cushion cover.

7 Carriage Way, Deptford Market Yard, SE8 4BZ
Nearest station: Deptford
freeweaver.info

30

M.Y.O

Rediscover the pleasures of childhood crafts

Why should crafty fun be reserved for kids? M.Y.O (Make Your Own) creators Diana Muendo and Sam Lehane left their corporate careers in 2017 to establish this place for adult creativity in a little corner of south London. Playful, easy-to-pick-up crafts are the speciality here, such as handmade pottery, metal embossing, lino printing and macramé. Inside, it's like a sweetshop, with polka dot tablecloths, jars of shiny sequins and beads, shelves of squashy pots and a dresser spilling with silky ribbons. Perfection is not the point in these casual classes, where tutors are happily hands-off. Bring a friend and a bottle (M.Y.O will lend you a glass) and recapture a bit of messy, juvenile joy.

82 Redcross Way, SE1 1HA
Nearest station: Borough
myo.place

31

THE BOTANICAL CAKE STUDIO

Cake decorations too pretty to eat

With a background as a chef and wedding cake maker, Clare Margary has found her calling creating extraordinary naturalistic flowers from sugar paste. Put aside thoughts of naff confections from the 1980s; Clare has honed a technique for crafting realistic decorative botanicals that embrace imperfection. In her garden studio, she'll take you through making a rose and sweet peas by cutting and working thin paste using pastry tools, then assembling them using egg white as glue. A final sprinkling of magical-sounding 'petal dust' will make the flat colours twinkle into life. Clare mostly teaches one-on-one sessions, so can tailor them to your interests, although you can also join one of her group classes.

109 Westdean Avenue, SE12 9NJ
Nearest station: Grove Park
thebotanicalcakestudio.com

32

THE RINGSMITHS

Create a one-of-a-kind token of affection

As making experiences go, this one's a gem. Create a bespoke ring for your significant other, a friend or yourself in the intimate courtyard behind edgy jewellers Kas & Ros. Owners Milena Kovanovic and Ros Millar teach you how to file and carve a form in blue jeweller's wax, before it gets sent away to be cast in silver. The candlelight isn't just for ambience; you can use a flame to give your ring a molten bubbly texture, or chip wax away for a rugged effect. Choose from lots of extras to make it truly yours, including engraving and setting with gemstones. If you're not a natural creative, fear not: these experienced jewellers will help you make something unique in no time.

61 Tower Bridge Road, SE1 4TL
Nearest station: London Bridge
Other location: Waterloo
theringsmiths.com

33

THE GOODLIFE CENTRE

Get on top of those pesky DIY tasks

Ever balked at the cost of tradesmen and wished you could do the job yourself? Then this place is for you. This quirky spot in an old cardboard box factory offers 60 practical lessons to empower people with handy skills. Experienced and patient tutors demystify drilling, tiling, plumbing and basic joinery, along with more creative pursuits like basketry and passementerie (making fringed tassels and trims). Behind it all is motivational powerhouse Alison Winfield-Chislett, who visits the classes mid-morning with a tea trolley and a pep talk. Don't be put off by the centre's slightly old-school premise – there's a wide range of punters here, from young homeowners (perfect housewarming gift alert) to CEOs who like to drop in and de-stress.

49/55 Great Guildford Street, SE1 0ES
Nearest station: Borough
thegoodlifecentre.co.uk

34

PAPER STORIES

Coffee with a side of collage

This neighbourhood cafe invites you to get crafty with collage. Just a fiver is enough to buy a kit of 'odds' (an envelope stuffed with coloured, textured and patterned paper scraps) and 'bods' (a joyous range of animal shapes and faces to stick the scraps onto). Everything you need to cut and paste is on your pre-booked table, including mini hole punches that make charming little hearts and stars. Paper Stories is a sure-fire hit with young children, but there are kits and activities geared for teens and adults, too. If an hour here gets you hooked on paper art, come back for a class in risograph printing or vision boarding. In this friendly space you could find a whole new tribe.

234 Gipsy Road, SE27 9BJ
Nearest station: Gipsy Hill
paper-stories.co.uk

35

ART4SPACE

Inner-city sanctuary offering craft as healing

The cost of learning a craft excludes many people – something this big-hearted Stockwell arts centre aims to remedy. Classes in mosaic, *kintsugi* (the Japanese art of repairing with gold), ceramics and textiles are reasonably priced and come with experienced tutors. Learning a skill here funds the centre's outreach work, aimed at deploying craft as a mental health therapy for more people. Themes of healing and repair won't be lost on you as you transform broken pottery into brilliant mirror art or sew scrap fabric into a scrunchie. It's not so much about what you make here as allowing yourself to enjoy the process. Quiet, table-based classes provide the perfect setting for conversation to flow.

Unit 1, 31 Jeffreys Road, SW4 6QU
Nearest station: Stockwell
art4space.co.uk

36

JAMJAR EDIT

Flower pressing, folklore and fashion gossip

A tip-filled two-hour class with fashion world florists JamJar revives a childhood craft favourite: the art of flower pressing is all grown up and still utterly charming. Set pretty stems between sheets of card and blotting paper, then squeeze it all together, sandwich-like, and screw into place. Choose delicate heads to ensure faithful preservations rather than disappointing brown mush when you open up your press weeks later. As you playfully arrange blossoms, you're regaled with the folklore of each species and amusing tales about the craft – and you'll hear a few fashion industry anecdotes too, *darling*. Take home your bursting flower press and two card-sized botanical artworks that you'll make using JamJar's archive.

10A Peacock Yard, Iliffe Street, SE17 3LH
Nearest stations: Elephant & Castle, Kennington
jamjaredit.co.uk

37

MAUREEN LUXE STUDIO

Cast a terrazzo coaster with craft resin

In a serene, greenhouse-like setting above Brixton Market, homeware designer Mo leads an easy-going class on casting terrazzo objects with jesmonite. This craft resin (simple to use, quick to dry and loved by hobbyists) comes in liquid and powder forms that set hard when mixed. To give your tray, coaster or candleholder bright flashes of colour, you'll first make colourful chips by swirling drops of pigment into the mix and spreading it out to dry. Crumble this dried mixture, sprinkle it into a plain mix, then pour it all into a mould. It's no more difficult than baking: the hardest part is patiently waiting to see how your custom pieces emerge.

The Black Farmer Farmshop,
25–27 Market Row, SW9 8LD
Nearest station: Brixton
maureenluxestudio.com

38

VARIEGATE

Tackle woodwork basics

If your primary motivation for learning a craft is to impress (no judgement here), then imagine the reaction when you serve up charcuterie on a hand-crafted board of your own making. In a small class of just three or four, two seasoned furniture makers will share their passion and empower you to creatively transform reclaimed ash or beech offcuts into a personal piece. You'll gain the confidence to use a bandsaw, sanding machines and a pillar drill to shape and finish your board. Top tip: novices should opt for freestyle designs that are more forgiving than precisely geometric ones. In just half a day, you'll have a smooth and chunky board that's oiled and ready for admiration at your next dinner party.

Private address
Nearest station: Southfields
variegate.uk

39

THE FIND STORE

Neighbourhood spot for painting pots

It began as a small but well-curated gift and coffee shop but the added offer of pottery painting has become so popular, it's practically taken over. Grab an apron and choose an item – there's everything from egg cups to olive bowls and cat figurines – to imbue with a colourful, artsy finish. Start with something small to keep the experience from getting expensive and bring the kids: all the dotting and dabbing has a calming effect on even the most boisterous, who can be bribed with hot chocolate if you need time to finish your own masterpiece. The store will fire your pieces to a glossy finish. By night, it also offers classes in wheel-throwing and sgraffito techniques (scratching surface layers for decorative effect)

133 Burnt Ash Road, SE12 8RA
Nearest station: Lee
thefindstore.co.uk

40

BONEYARD LONDON

Have a bash at blacksmithing

Humans have been whacking hot metal into shapes since 6000 BCE, so don't be surprised if you feel a primal urge here. You'll heat stainless steel under a flame until it glows and repeatedly hammer it into shape on an anvil to form a rugged kitchen knife or wizard's wand. This isn't about brute strength but technique, something to have fun experimenting with over a few hours of hard hitting. Boneyard's offer is not the usual tourist experience, where an expert takes over the hard parts. You'll be expected to get stuck in at all stages, using power tools to decorate and finish. The forge is hot, the tools are heavy and you may get blisters, but it's a thrill to be outside your comfort zone.

Railway Arches, Pope's Grove, TW1 4JW
Nearest station: Strawberry Hill
boneyardlondon.com

41

PIGMENT PRESS

Make your own merch

Behind Shepherd Bush Market's stalls of stinky fish and gold bling is a silkscreen print studio making giant banners for local businesses. Here, you can learn how to transfer a photo or artwork onto T-shirts in a day. You'll first coat and expose a screen to create a stencil, then mix up a custom colour of satisfyingly squidgy ink to squeeze through it onto five white cotton tees. This happens on a carousel, where the screen stays put while the shirts are rotated underneath to make five exact copies – your very own line of custom T-shirts. Come back for Print Club Soda, a monthly night of poster printing with cocktails and pizza from The Hawk's Nest.

Arch 182, Shepherd's Bush Market, W12 8DF
Nearest station: Shepherd's Bush Market
pigmentpress.co.uk

42

EARL OF EAST

Short and sweet candle-making class

If you've ever suspected that scented candles are overhyped, let this crash course in wax-based wizardry convince you otherwise. Spend an hour with an expert in the lab-like space behind the brand's compact store learning how fragrances affect our feelings, before pouring your own candle. While happily tinkering with glass beakers and test tubes, you'll first make a blend from eight scents – including citrusy neroli and earthy oud. Mix this with hot soy wax and pour into a sleek 6oz amber jar, labelling your creation with its own name. While your candle sets, enjoy an excellent coffee in store, browse the scandi-influenced homewares (class attendees get a discount) or glean more pro tips, like how to extend the life of your candle by trimming the wick.

Unit 2, Quadrant Arcade, W1B 5RL
Nearest station: Piccadilly Circus
earlofeast.com

43

STUDIO POTTERY LONDON

Stress-free way to work with clay

If you take a spot in the picture window of this chic ceramics studio, know that you will be an attraction for Belgravia's passing tourists. For those that don't mind spectators, a wheel-throwing class here helps you work rapidly through the steps of centring a clay lump, opening a hole in it with your thumbs and squeezing the sides up into a basic cylinder or bowl. If your first effort is a no-go, you're encouraged to dump it and try again (unfired clay is infinitely recyclable). Repeat as necessary to reach a satisfying result. Your best pot goes off to be fired and glazed in a glossy dark green, ready for pickup a few weeks later.

29 Eccleston Place, SW1W 9NF
Nearest station: Victoria
studio-pottery-london.com

44

FULHAM TEXTILE STUDIO

Knit a beanie the easy way

For craft without the graft, a circular knitting machine could be your new best friend. Turning the handle on this nifty bit of kit makes a ring of plastic needles bob up and down, doing the work of picking up yarn and locking it into circular rows of stitch for you. It's so easy that it almost feels like cheating. The friendly, chatty instructors will show you how to use it to make a beanie in a thick flecked or brightly coloured yarn of your choice. Help is on hand if you become unstuck or go off track – entirely possible if the welcome drink or chatter here gets you *too* relaxed. Walk out proud with something you made yourself – no one need know exactly how.

2 Argon Mews, SW6 1BJ
Nearest station: Fulham Broadway
fulhamtextilestudio.com

45

RAY STITCH

Sew much fun in Islington

There's something about sewing machines that can bring out stress, but mistakes are met with laughs and friendly encouragement at Ray Stitch's introductory class, where patient tutors help you to feel 'at one' with your beginner-friendly machine. Starting with the basics of winding the bobbin and threading the needle, you'll emerge with an impressive tote bag (*with pockets!*) made in a cool fabric of your choosing. As with TV's *The Great British Sewing Bee*, camaraderie emerges as you navigate common pitfalls, muddle through missteps and congratulate each other on your results. While you beaver away in the basement, it's business as usual in the stylish and sought-out haberdashery above, so you can stock up on supplies if you've got the sewing bug.

66 Essex Road, N1 8LR
Nearest station: Essex Road
raystitch.co.uk

46

RAINBOW GLASS STUDIOS

Be dazzled by a stained-glass guru

Hear a crack at any time on this day-long stained-glass course and it needn't spell disaster. With an impressive 25 years of experience, Richard Paton has many tricks up his sleeve to fix almost any mishap. At his jewel-box Stokey studio, learn how to make an A4 panel to your own design, from selecting and cutting glass offcuts in sweet-wrapper colours, to hand-shaping lead bars around them and soldering the joins with a scorching hot iron. It's intense work, requiring just the right amount of pressure to handle the glass without it breaking (but fret not: there's a special glue in case it does). Make it through unscathed and the results are heavenly: a luminous artwork and a gratifying glimpse into this historic craft.

172 Stoke Newington Church Street, N16 0JL
Nearest station: Stoke Newington
rainbowglassstudios.co.uk

47

SLIPSTITCH

LGBTQ+ friendly yarn shop with classes

Author and stitch fanatic Rosie Fletcher really wants you to knit – or at least to not be stressed trying. She'll take you through a three-hour class at her bright and welcoming yarn shop, where there are 'no silly questions'. You'll make a mug cosy (or a coaster if you're here to crochet) while learning to cast on and off, knit and purl. Quiet concentration unravels in the third hour as classmates relax into it and the chat starts to flow. If you're keen for more, come back for the equally relaxed Fair Isle jumper, cardigan and sock-making courses. Monthly queer craft socials make this lively knit hub one of the city's most inclusive.

108 Alexandra Park Road, N10 2AE
Nearest station: Bounds Green
slipstitchldn.co.uk

48

THE FLOWER APPRECIATION SOCIETY

Grow the confidence to arrange wild blooms

There's something instantly relaxing about this cottage-like floristry studio in the hinterlands of De Beauvoir Town. Beginners are offered an abundance of high-quality seasonal blooms, some from the studio's own cutting garden, to arrange into a bouquet or low vase – along with a glass of fizz. First, you'll be shown how to condition your flowers for longevity by stripping away lower leaves, leaving a long, clean stem. Your tutor then reveals trade tips for proportioning fillers, foliage and 'big heads' (roses, tulips and rarer species) to achieve a wild and whimsical English garden style. Knowing when to stop the floral fussing can be tough, but you'll be helped to reach a satisfying stage without overdoing it.

72A Southgate Road, N1 3JF
Nearest station: Haggerston
theflowerappreciationsociety.co.uk

49

TURNING EARTH HIGHGATE

Beginner classes in clay

This is among the city's more established places to learn ceramics, consistently popular thanks to its laid-back vibe and spacious workshops festooned with hanging plants. Beginner classes at each of the three locations aim to get you independent enough to carry on your own practice (it takes something like 10,000 hours to become a master potter, after all). You'll learn to prep clay and raise a cylinder on the wheel after a tutor demonstrates. Watch closely, as the process is much trickier when you attempt it yourself. You should end up with a decent result within a morning, but if not, the peaceful and positive atmosphere here will compel you to return for another try.

Woodside Works, Summersby Road, N6 5UH
Nearest station: Highgate
Other locations: Hoxton, Leyton
turningearth.org

50

LONDON SCHOOL OF MOSAIC

Assemble an artwork of tiny tiles

Tucked beneath a Gospel Oak housing block, London School of Mosaic welcomes would-be pixellators to learn this ancient art form in a day. You'll first be taught how to translate your original design into key mosaic shapes (tesserae, to be exact): square, half-square and keystone. Then choose your palette from a pick-and-mix of tiles in traditional ceramic or glittery coloured glass, nip these into shape with a hand tool, then glue them piece by piece onto a wooden base before grouting. Sustained concentration is required if you're aiming for a level of precision that would please a Roman artisan. Keep yourself fuelled at Mother Canteen next door: a community cafe serving hot stews and other hearty fare.

181 Mansfield Road, NW3 2HP
Nearest station: Gospel Oak
lsomosaic.com

51

SEWINGSMITH

Extend the life of beloved garments

Shelley Zetuni's past life involved making hats for the Royals, but she now applies her nimble fingers to mending clothes with delightfully neat embroidery. In her regular classes, she shares how to creatively repair denim, wool and linen, working with colourful thread and a darning disc to help secure the fabric as you patch. If your freehand skills are lacking, try a Speedweve – a tiny loom that easily makes quick and strong mends you can proudly display. Start with practice swatches rather than your most cherished items, as mastering this skill requires a few tries. Once you're in the darning habit, you'll be rummaging in the back of your wardrobe for more items to fix.

The Busworks, United House, North Road, N7 9DP
Nearest station: Caledonian Road
sewingsmith.co.uk

52

CUBITTS

Make your own spectacles

If you're obsessive about specs and want bragging rights on your next pair, make your own at Cubitts HQ. The cult eyewear brand builds on London's long association with the trade, employing traditional and modern processes. You'll spend a lot of time filing, sanding and shaping an acetate template that's been tailored especially to you. More fiddly jobs involve creating grooves for the lenses, punching out the nose bridge and inlaying hinges. There's only so much a layman can do, so at the halfway stage a technician takes your frames to be tumbled in a barrel of woodchips for a buff and polish, then they're finessed by Cubitts and sent to you 3–4 weeks later. This class is pricey, but does include the cost of your frames.

55–61 Brewery Road, N7 9QH
Nearest station: Caledonian Road & Barnsbury
cubitts.com

53

LOOP

Masterclass mecca for knitting fans

There's barely space to cross your knitting needles in this compact yarn shop full of grandmotherly charm, where classes are squeezed in among bundles of luxury yarns, books and vintage haberdashery. Knit and crochet beginners are handled patiently on Loop's sell-out introductory classes, but for those with some know-how, the masterclasses – led by artist-teachers from around the world – are unbeatable. Darning superstar Celia Pym teaches a regular Saturday workshop here, while others on the ever-changing roster include experts in stitching folk art, embroidering florals and creating costumes for soft toys.

15 Camden Passage, N1 8EA
Nearest station: Angel
loopknitting.com

54

QUILT CLUB

Stitch your part of something bigger

This free club welcomes everyone, whether you want to learn to make your own quilt or to contribute a square for a larger project. It happens weekly in an old city-fringes warehouse that's become part of a thriving grassroots creative community. It's full of friendly faces, so don't be shy in asking others to help you get started. Rock up to a sewing machine and grab a pattern and some fabric (donated from the local rag trade). Easy to learn and fun to do in groups, quilting has a rich history as a community art form and it's also ripe for making statements: Quilt Club's calling card is to shroud whole buildings in quilts as a celebration of diversity in the local area.

195 Eade Road, N4 1DN
Nearest station: Manor House
quiltclub.co.uk

55

ROSEUR

Breathtaking bouquets

Big and dramatic is how this sculptural florist likes its arrangements. Roseur's hand-tied bouquet class starts with the basics of working with colour, line and form, before imparting some hot tips on how to give blooms maximum wow factor. Dried flowers are a speciality here – a 1970s trend that's back thanks to its planet-friendly credentials. Gathering chosen stems into one hand, you'll add florals and foliage one by one into a spiral. Keep a tight grip, as unruly leaves and tangling flower heads will resist your attempts at order. A floor-length mirror allows you to assess your bouquet from all angles – you can play at being a bride, checking out how your bouquet looks to guests.

Unit 112, Lower Stable Street, Coal Drops Yard, N1C 4DR
Nearest station: King's Cross St Pancras
roseur.co.uk

IMAGE CREDITS

An Opinionated Guide to Make London
First edition

Published in 2025 by
Hoxton Mini Press, London
Copyright © Hoxton Mini Press 2025.
All rights reserved.

Text by Riya Patel
Editing by Zoë Jellicoe and
    Gaynor Sermon
Production design by Dom Grant
Production control by David Brimble
Proofreading by Florence Ward
Editorial support by Richard Enright

With thanks to Matthew Young for
initial series design.

Please note: we recommend checking
the websites listed for each entry
before you visit for the latest
information on price, opening times
and pre-booking requirements.

The right of Riya Patel to be identified
as the creator of this Work has been
asserted under the Copyright, Designs
and Patents Act 1988.

Thank you to all of the individuals
and institutions who have provided
images and arranged permissions.
While every effort has been made to
trace the present copyright holders we
apologise in advance for any
unintentional omission or error, and
would be pleased to insert the
appropriate acknowledgement in any
subsequent edition.

A CIP catalogue record for this book is
available from the British Library.

ISBN: 978-1-914314-98-8

Printed and bound by OZGraf, Poland

Manufacturer: Hoxton Mini Press, 104
Northside Studios, 16–29 Andrews
Road, London E8 4QF, UK
www.hoxtonminipress.com

Represented by: Authorised Rep
Compliance Ltd., Ground Floor,
71 Lower Baggot Street,
Dublin D02 P593, Ireland
www.arccompliance.com

Hoxton Mini Press is an environmen-
tally conscious publisher, committed
to offsetting our carbon footprint.
This book is 100 per cent carbon
compensated, with offset purchased
from Stand For Trees.

Every time you order from our website,
we plant a tree:
www.hoxtonminipress.com

MIX
Paper | Supporting
responsible forestry
FSC® C163799

Selected opinionated guides in the series:

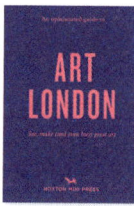

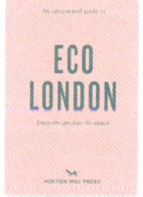

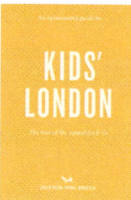

For more go to www.hoxtonminipress.com

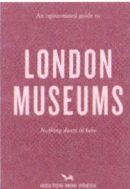

TYPES OF CRAFT

Baking & cake decorating
  E5 Bakehouse, *13*
  The Botanical Cake Studio, *31*

Basketry
  The Goodlife Centre, *33*

Bookbinding
  Tea and Crafting, *4*
  London Centre for Book Arts, *6*

Distilling
  58 and CO, *18*

DIY skills
  The Goodlife Centre, *33*

Embroidery
  Tea and Crafting, *4*
  The London Embroidery Studio, *21*

Eyewear
  Cubitts, *52*

Flower pressing & arranging
  JamJar Edit, *36*
  The Flower Appreciation Society, *48*
  Roseur, *55*

Gardening
  London Terrariums, *17*

Glassblowing
  Gather, *27*

Jesmonite casting
  Maureen Luxe Studio, *37*

Jewellery
  The Ringsmiths, *32*

Knitting & crochet
  Tea and Crafting, *4*
  Fulham Textile Studio, *44*
  Slipstich, *47*
  Loop, *53*

Leathercraft
  Pophams Home, *16*
  Yussico, *23*

Macramé
  Tea and Crafting, *4*
  M.Y.O, *30*

Metalwork
  Blackhorse Workshop, *8*
  Boneyard London, *40*

Mosaic
  Art4Space, *35*
  London School of Mosaic, *50*

Papercraft & collage
  Marmor Paperie, *25*
  The Fan Museum, *28*
  Paper Stories, *34*

Perfume
  Maya Njie, *1*

Pottery
  Cone8 Ceramics Studio, *11*
  Crown Works Pottery, *14*
  Kinboru Studios, *15*
  Pophams Home, *16*
  County Hall Pottery, *26*
  M.Y.O, *30*
  Art4Space, *35*
  The Find Store, *39*
  Studio Pottery London, *43*
  Turning Earth Highgate, *49*

Printing
  St Bride Foundation, *3*
  Tea and Crafting, *4*
  Print Club London, *7*
  M.Y.O, *30*
  Pigment Press, *41*

Sewing
  The New Craft House, *9*
  Art4Space, *35*
  Ray Stitch, *45*
  Sewingsmith, *51*
  Quilt Club, *54*

Stained-glass
  Rainbow Glass Studios, *46*

Stone carving
  London Stone Carving, *24*

Straw marquetry
  Kim Jordan, *20*

Tufting
  Tufting London, *22*
  Fulham Textile Studio, *44*

Wax casting & candle-making
  Pophams Home, *16*
  Wax Atelier, *19*
  Earl of East, *42*

Weaving
  Dalia James, *5*
  Freeweaver Studio, *29*

Woodwork
  Clunie Fretton, *2*
  Blackhorse Workshop, *8*
  The Green Wood Guild, *10*
  New School of Furniture
    Making, *12*
  The Goodlife Centre, *33*
  Variegate, *38*

INDEX

58 and CO, *18*

Art4Space, *35*

Blackhorse Workshop, *8*

Boneyard London, *40*

The Botanical Cake Studio, *31*

Clunie Fretton, *2*

Cone8 Ceramics Studio, *11*

County Hall Pottery, *26*

Crown Works Pottery, *14*

Cubitts, *52*

Dalia James, *5*

E5 Bakehouse, *13*

Earl of East, *42*

The Fan Museum, *28*

The Find Store, *39*

The Flower Appreciation Society, *48*

Freeweaver Studio, *29*

Fulham Textile Studio, *44*

Gather, *27*

The Goodlife Centre, *33*

The Green Wood Guild, *10*

JamJar Edit, *36*

Kim Jordan, *20*

Kinboru Studios, *15*

London Centre for Book Arts, *6*

The London Embroidery Studio, *21*

London School of Mosaic, *50*

London Stone Carving, *24*

London Terrariums, *17*

Loop, *53*

M.Y.O, *30*

Marmor Paperie, *25*

Maureen Luxe Studio, *37*

Maya Njie, *1*

New School of
    Furniture Making, *12*

Paper Stories, *34*

Pigment Press, *41*

Pophams Home, *16*

Print Club London, *7*

Quilt Club, *54*

Rainbow Glass Studios, *46*

Ray Stitch, *45*

Roseur, *55*

Sewingsmith, *51*

Slipstich, *47*

St Bride Foundation, *3*

Studio Pottery London, *43*

Tea and Crafting, *4*

The New Craft House, *9*

The Ringsmiths, *32*

Tufting London, *22*

Turning Earth Highgate, *49*

Variegate, *38*

Wax Atelier, *19*

Yussico, *23*